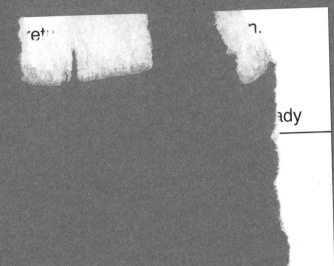

Usborne
GREEK MYTHS
PICTURE BOOK

ROSIE DICKINS

ANCIENT GREEK EXPERT: PROFESSOR VERITY PLATT

ILLUSTRATED BY GALIA BERNSTEIN AND DESIGNED BY NICOLA BUTLER

CONTENTS

NOTE ON NAMES:

The Greek myths were so popular, they were adopted by the Romans – who often gave the characters Roman names. This book uses the original Greek names, which you can see below with their Roman equivalents (*in italics*).

Aphrodite - *Venus*

Ares - *Mars*

Artemis - *Diana*

Athena - *Minerva*

Cronus - *Saturn*

Demeter - *Ceres*

Dionysus - *Bacchus*

Eros - *Cupid*

Hades - *Pluto*

Hephaestus - *Vulcan*

Hera - *Juno*

Heracles - *Hercules*

Hermes - *Mercury*

Hestia - *Vesta*

Persephone - *Proserpina*

Poseidon - *Neptune*

Odysseus - *Ulysses*

Zeus - *Jupiter*

To hear how to say Greek names, and for links to websites where you can find out more about Greek myths and ancient Greece, go to www.usborne.com/quicklinks and type in the keywords 'greek myths picture book'.

*When a date includes the letters BC, it means it is from the time before the birth of Christ, over 2,000 years ago. Dates in this period are counted backwards – so bigger numbers mean longer ago.

BEGINNING OF THE MYTHS

OVER TWO THOUSAND YEARS AGO in ancient Greece, people told each other thrilling tales of gods and heroes. These stories, known as the Greek myths, have been told and retold ever since.

To the Ancient Greeks, the myths were more than just stories. They were a part of their history and religion, and explained how the world and its many gods came to be.

Greek bowls and vases were often decorated with beautiful paintings, including scenes from the myths.

PAINTED VASE
Greek vase showing a warrior on horseback, 6th century BC*

The most important gods lived on top of Mount Olympus, the highest mountain in Greece – seen here in a modern photo.

BIRTH OF VENUS
15th-century Italian painting by Sandro Botticelli

This famous painting shows Aphrodite, Greek goddess of love – whose Roman name was 'Venus'.

The ancient Greeks made beautiful paintings and sculptures about their myths, and many of these still survive. Other famous artworks were created centuries later – and the myths continue to inspire artists today.

This book includes a selection from throughout the ages.

The ancient Greeks built magnificent temples for their gods, decorated with statues and carvings, and some remains still stand. This site, known as the Athens Acropolis, contains some of the most famous.

THE TITANS

ACCORDING TO THE GREEK MYTHS, the gods were descended from a race of giants known as the Titans.

The Titans towered over the world.

The Titans were the children of the Earth and the Sky. Huge, handsome and powerful, they ruled the world during a long-ago golden age.

FOUNTAIN OF CRONUS
Detail from 17th-century French sculpture. This gold-covered Cronus was made for a royal palace.

The time of the Titans was a time of peace and plenty.

The chief Titan, Cronus, knew he would be overthrown by one of his children. So he swallowed them as soon as they were born. Eventually his wife Rhea tricked him into sparing one, by giving him a stone wrapped in a blanket to swallow instead.

The child Cronus didn't swallow was named Zeus. When Zeus grew up, he forced Cronus to spit out his other children. These children became the first Greek gods. They wrested control of the world from the Titans in a battle that lasted ten years.

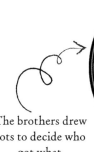

The brothers drew lots to decide who got what.

After defeating the Titans, Zeus and his brothers divided the world between them. Zeus took the Sky, Poseidon the Seas, and Hades the underground realm known as the Underworld. The Earth they agreed to share.

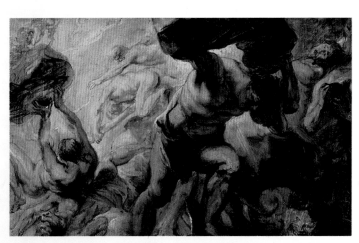

This painting shows the end of the battle, with the Titans falling or fleeing before the gods.

THE FALL OF THE TITANS
17th-century Flemish painting by Peter Paul Rubens

Not all of Earth's children were as handsome as the Titans. There was also a race of one-eyed giants known as Cyclopes – and others so ugly, they hid away underground.

This is how one 19th-century artist imagined a Cyclops. (The plural of Cyclops is Cyclopes.)

THE CYCLOPS
19th-century French painting by Odilon Redon

ATLAS

Atlas was an incredibly strong Titan. He led the Titans in their battle with the gods. When Zeus won, he punished Atlas by making him hold up the heavens. Eventually, Atlas turned to stone and became the Atlas Mountains.

This statue – a Roman copy of a Greek original – shows Atlas with the heavens weighing on his shoulders.

ATLAS
Roman statue, 3rd century

The High Atlas Mountains as they look today

PROMETHEUS

Prometheus was a clever Titan who stole fire from the gods and gave it to people. Zeus punished him by chaining him up with an eagle pecking at his liver – until Zeus's son, Heracles, rescued him.

Although their punishments were harsh, Prometheus and Atlas couldn't die because Titans were immortal and lived forever.

Prometheus (second from left) hid the fire inside a hollow stalk, which he is holding here.

PROMETHEUS AND SATYRS
Detail from Greek vase, 5th century BC

ATLAS AND PROMETHEUS
Greek cup, 6th century BC

THE FIRST GODS

THE FIRST GODS were the children of the Titans.
There were three brothers: Zeus, Poseidon and Hades,
and three sisters: Hera, Hestia and Demeter.
These six were soon joined by more.

ZEUS AND THE EAGLE
Greek cup, 6th century BC

ZEUS

Mighty Zeus was the King of
the Gods. He was the god of the sky
and hurled magical thunderbolts when
angry. He was often pictured with certain
symbols: thunderbolts, an eagle and an
oak tree, to help people to recognize him.

Zeus could change shape and become anything from a
bedraggled cuckoo to a powerful swan – especially if it
helped to impress a woman (he was always falling in love).

Poseidon could use his
trident to stir up storms.

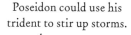

HADES

Hades was the god of the
Underworld, the kingdom of the
dead. His symbols were a helmet
that made the wearer invisible, and his
three-headed dog, Cerberus.

HADES
Detail from 16th-century Flemish
painting by Peter Paul Rubens

POSEIDON

Poseidon was the god of the sea and lived in a
palace below the waves. He carried a three-pronged
trident that was one of his symbols. He was often
shown with dolphins and horses, and created
the first horse as a gift to the Greeks.

POSEIDON CALMING THE WAVES
18th-century French statue by Lambert-Sigisbert Adam

HESTIA

Kind and peace-loving,
Hestia was goddess
of home and hearth.
She had few adventures,
and was usually shown
wrapped in a veil.

HERA WITH A PEACOCK
Detail from 16th-century Italian fresco
by Baldassarre Peruzzi

HERA

Hera was the wife of Zeus, and the goddess of women and marriage. Her symbols were a sceptre (a staff representing power) and peacocks. She was said to have put the eyes in the peacock's tail.

APHRODITE

Beautiful Aphrodite was born out of the sea, like a pearl, and became the goddess of love. Her symbols included roses and doves. Flowers sprang up where she walked.

Aphrodite's son, Eros, shot magic arrows that made people fall in love.

This statue once had arms, and was painted and decked in jewels.

APHRODITE
Greek marble statue, 2nd century BC

DEMETER

Demeter was the goddess of nature and harvests, and was said to have taught people how to grow crops. Her symbol was a wheatsheaf.

DEMETER WITH TRIPTOLEMUS
Detail from Greek vase, 5th century BC

Demeter gives a young prince seeds and a winged chariot.

The gods often argued. In one dispute, Hera, Aphrodite and Zeus' daughter, Athena, all claimed to be the best-looking. They asked a prince named Paris to decide – and offered him bribes to win.

Paris awarded a golden apple to the fairest goddess.

Paris chose Aphrodite, who had promised him the love of the world's most beautiful woman, Helen of Troy (see page 28).

THE JUDGEMENT OF PARIS
15th-century Italian painting by an unknown artist

CHILDREN OF ZEUS

ZEUS HAD MANY CHILDREN with many different mothers. All of his children had special powers and several became gods themselves.

ATHENA

Athena sprang fully-grown from Zeus's head. Powerful and wise, she became the goddess of wisdom, war and weaving. She was rarely seen without her helmet, and her symbols were an owl and an olive tree.

ATHENA
Greek coin,
5th century BC

Athena was patron of the city of Athens, and her picture appeared on the city's coins.

PALLAS ATHENA
19th-century Austrian painting by Gustav Klimt
(Athena was sometimes given the extra name Pallas.)

APOLLO

Golden-haired Apollo was a brilliant musician, the god of the Sun, light and truth. His symbol was a laurel tree.

Apollo's golden good looks were supposed to represent perfect beauty.

APOLLO
15th-century Italian ceiling painting
by Pietro Perugino

ARTEMIS

Dark-haired Artemis was the goddess of hunting and the Moon, and she also protected young girls. She is often shown carrying a bow and arrows, and accompanied by a deer.

Apollo and Artemis were twins and are often pictured together.

ARTEMIS THE HUNTRESS
Roman wall painting,
1st century BC

APOLLO AND ARTEMIS WITH A DEER
Greek vase, 5th century BC

8

HEPHAESTUS

Hard-working Hephaestus was the gods' blacksmith. A powerful man who walked with a limp, he could make amazing weapons and other magical objects.

Some said Hephaestus worked at the heart of a volcano.

ARES

Ares was a god of war. He was strong and handsome, but had a terrible temper. His symbols included weapons, dogs and vultures.

Ares was god of the bloodthirsty side of war, while Athena looked after strategy.

ARES
Roman copy of a Greek original,
4th century BC

HERMES

Quick and clever, Hermes grew up to become the gods' messenger. You can recognize him by his winged sandals.

The sandals – made by Hephaestus – allowed Hermes to fly through the air.

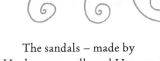

HERMES
Detail from Greek vase,
5th century BC

Hermes was a precocious baby. The day he was born, he stole a herd of sacred cattle and invented the lyre – a musical instrument a bit like a harp – which he then gave to Apollo.

DIONYSUS

Dionysus was born from Zeus's thigh, and became the god of wine and merry-making. He usually wore a crown of vine leaves.

After Dionysus discovered the secret of wine-making, he wandered the world, teaching it to people.

Dionysus was said to travel in a chariot pulled by wild beasts.

HEROES

GREEK MYTHS TELL MANY TALES of heroic men and women, bravely battling their enemies.

THESEUS

Prince Theseus saved his people from the man-eating Minotaur. Half-man, half-bull, the Minotaur lurked deep inside a labyrinth. A princess named Ariadne gave Theseus a sword, and a ball of thread to help him find his way out.

THESEUS SLAYING THE MINOTAUR
19th-century French sculpture
by Antoine Barye

HERACLES

The son of Zeus and a mortal woman, Heracles was famously strong. As a baby, he strangled snakes in his cradle. When he grew up, he performed many heroic deeds, known as the Twelve Tasks (see pages 22-23).

THE INFANT HERACLES
Roman statue, date unknown

Heracles was half-immortal and later joined the gods above Mount Olympus. He became the god of heroes and athletes.

PERSEUS

Perseus was another son of Zeus. He killed a snake-haired monster called Medusa (see page 13). Her gaze turned people to stone, so he couldn't look at her directly. Instead, he used the reflection in his shield.

Perseus flew through the sky with the help of winged sandals.

After killing Medusa, Perseus rescued Princess Andromeda from a deadly sea monster – as seen in this detail from the painting on the right – and then married her.

PERSEUS RESCUING ANDROMEDA
16th-century Italian painting by Piero di Cosimo

BELLEROPHON

Bellerophon accomplished many daring deeds. Most famously, he tamed Pegasus, the winged horse, and killed a fire-breathing monster known as the Chimera (see page 13).

BELLEROPHON RIDING PEGASUS
17th-century Flemish painting by Peter Paul Rubens

The Chimera was immune to ordinary weapons. Instead, Bellerophon put a lump of lead on his spear. The lead melted in the monster's fiery breath and killed it.

ATALANTA

Atalanta was a wild huntress who could run faster and shoot better than almost anyone. She had many adventures, including sailing with Jason (see page 20) in search of the magical golden fleece.

ATALANTA
Greek statue, 2nd century

Atalanta was born a princess, but raised by wild bears.

ACHILLES

Fearless Achilles was a Greek warrior and hero of the Trojan War (see page 28). He was almost immune to injury. His only weak spot was his heel – which is where the phrase "Achilles' heel" comes from.

Some say Achilles gained his strength by being dipped in the River Styx as a baby.

PSYCHE

Psyche was so beautiful, she made Aphrodite jealous. When Eros fell in love with Psyche, Aphrodite tried to keep them apart by setting Psyche a series of almost impossible tasks. But Psyche succeeded, became a goddess and lived happily ever after with Eros.

① ② ③ ④

THE TASKS OF PSYCHE
19th-century English painting by John Stanhope

To the ancient Greeks, Psyche represented the human soul.

① Psyche had to separate a basket of grains...

② ...gather wool from deadly sheep...

③ ...collect water from a stream guarded by serpents...

④ ...and bring back a box from the Underworld.

MONSTERS

THE MYTHS DESCRIBE SOME TERRIBLE MONSTERS:
man-eating, fire-breathing monstrosities. Other monsters looked more human, but were just as scary.

TYPHON

Typhon was the first monster. As tall as the sky, he was part human and part dragon, with a hundred heads, and eyes that flashed fire. His children included the Sphinx and the Chimera.

TYPHON
Detail from Greek vase, 6th century BC

Typhon almost overthrew Zeus. After a violent fight, Zeus trapped him under Mount Etna (a volcano in Sicily), where he continued to rumble dangerously.

Some artists showed Typhon with just one human head and some with more. His other heads were those of dragons.

GRAEAE

The Graeae were three old crones who had only one eye and one tooth, which they passed between them.

Perseus once stole the crones' eye and refused to give it back until they told him where to find Medusa.

SPHINX

A winged lion with a human head, the Sphinx challenged passersby to a riddle – and killed anyone who gave a wrong answer. It threw itself off a cliff after a prince named Oedipus solved the riddle.

SPHINX
Roman stone sculpture, date unknown

> WHAT GOES ON FOUR LEGS IN THE MORNING, TWO LEGS AT MIDDAY AND THREE LEGS IN THE EVENING?*

FURIES

The Furies were goddesses of vengeance. They had wings, eyes that dripped blood, and snakes for hair.

FURY
Detail from Etruscan vase, 4th century BC

*ANSWER: MAN (A BABY CRAWLS, A GROWN MAN WALKS ON TWO LEGS, AND AN OLD MAN WALKS WITH A STICK.)

THE FATES

The daughters of Night, the Fates controlled life and death.
Clotho spun the thread of life, Lachesis measured it out,
and Atropos cut it. Even the gods feared them.

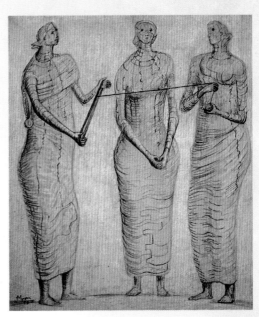

The Fates were
supposed to visit
children shortly after
birth, to predict
their destiny.

THE THREE FATES
20th-century English drawing by Henry Moore

MEDUSA
16th-century Italian shield
painting by Caravaggio

MEDUSA

Medusa had snakes for hair
and her gaze turned living
creatures to stone. She was
one of three terrifying sisters
known as the Gorgons.

In ancient Greece, gorgons' faces decorated
temples, houses and shields, in the belief
that they would ward off evil.

MINOTAUR

The Minotaur was a man-eating monster,
half man and half bull. It was kept locked
away in a labyrinth by King Minos of Crete,
who fed it with victims from nearby Athens
– until Theseus came along (see page 10).

CHIMERA

The Chimera was a fearsome
three-headed monster – part
lion, part goat and part snake –
which breathed fire. Seeing it was
an omen of storms and disasters.

CHIMERA OF AREZZO
Etruscan bronze, 4th century BC

The Chimera brought misery
to Lycia (now in southern
Turkey) until it was killed by
Bellerophon (see page 11).

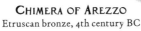

13

Magical Beings

The Greek myths were full of weird and wonderful animals and other magical beings – from fierce griffins to the famous flying horse, Pegasus.

The Three Graces

The Three Graces were goddesses of charm and beauty. Sometimes they were said to be servants of Aphrodite. They were usually shown holding hands and dancing.

SPRING - DETAIL OF THE THREE GRACES
15th-century Italian painting
by Sandro Botticelli

Griffins

Griffins were fierce, proud beasts, with the body of a lion, and the wings and head of an eagle. They were said to guard gold.

GRIFFIN'S HEAD
Greek, 7th century BC

Long after Greek times, Griffins were used on coats of arms as a symbol of bravery.

Centaurs

Centaurs were half-man, half-horse. Some were wild and untamed; others were wise and became famous teachers. The hero Achilles (see page 11) was taught to fight by a centaur.

The centaurs were formidable warriors.

This smiling statue was found in the villa of a Roman emperor. Notice the rough-looking club over one shoulder, a reminder of the centaur's fiercer side.

YOUNG CENTAUR
Roman bronze sculpture, 2nd century

SATYRS

Satyrs – also known as fauns by the Romans – were mischievous, pleasure-loving, wild creatures. They were usually shown with pointy ears, horns and hooves.

FAUN
18th-century French sculpture

Satyrs lived in forests and woods, and loved music and dancing.

THE MUSES

The Muses were nine daughters of Zeus, who helped inspire humans to create art – including music, poetry and plays.

THE MUSES
Roman mosaic, 4th century AD

Bellerophon later tried to fly Pegasus up to Mount Olympus. He fell off, but Pegasus joined the gods.

PEGASUS

Pegasus was a magical winged horse. He was said to inspire poets and, wherever he stamped his hoof, a spring bubbled up. He was tamed with a golden bridle by the hero Bellerophon (see page 11).

PEGASUS
19th-century French painting by Odilon Redon

HIPPOCAMPI

Hippocampi were the horses of the sea – usually shown with fishy tails. They pulled Poseidon's chariot through the waves.

The Greeks used to say the white crests on waves were the manes of Poseidon's horses.

THE WORLD OF THE MYTHS

THE WORLD OF THE MYTHS was an enchanted place, with gods and spirits in everything from the Sun and Moon to the rivers and winds.

HELIOS

Helios drove the Sun across the sky in a blazing chariot. At night, he sailed back over the ocean in a golden bowl.

SELENE

The Moon goddess Selene followed Helios across the sky at night, her radiant crown lighting up the dark.

PAN

Pan was the god of wild places. Part-man, part-goat, he carried a set of reed pipes known as pan pipes. He made the pipes in memory of a water nymph, who became a reed to hide from him.

NYMPHS

Female spirits called nymphs took care of different kinds of places. Tree nymphs were called dryads, and water nymphs were naiads.

Each spring or stream had its own naiad.

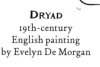

DRYAD
19th-century
English painting
by Evelyn De Morgan

PAN
16th-century Italian painting,
by Annibale Carracci

The middle or "navel" of the world was marked by a sacred stone – said to be the one Cronus swallowed instead of Zeus. The Greeks thought this stone was a route for speaking to the gods.

NAVEL STONE
Greek carved stone, 4th century BC

According to myth, many characters ended up among the stars – placed there by the gods, to ensure their memory lived forever. Even today, some constellations still have their names.

The star map below combines characters from many of the myths in this book – shown in the details around the edges.

The hero Perseus and Andromeda, the princess he rescued from a sea monster, along with Andromeda's mother

A fearsome lion fought by Heracles

The crown of Ariadne, the princess who helped Theseus defeat the Minotaur

A swan, one of Zeus's disguises

The hero Heracles with his club raised, ready to attack a many-headed monster

Pegasus, the winged horse

MAP OF THE NORTHERN CONSTELLATIONS
18th-century English print, by James Thornhill

ZEPHYRUS

Zephyrus was the god of the West wind. His gentle breath brought the spring. Boreas, his bad-tempered brother, was god of the wintry North wind.

**BIRTH OF VENUS –
DETAIL OF ZEPHYRUS AND AURA**
15th-century Italian painting by Botticelli
(Aura was the breeze)

Boreas is usually shown as an old man with shaggy hair and wings.

17

THE UNDERWORLD

IN THE GREEK MYTHS, the Underworld was a spooky underground kingdom, ruled by Zeus' brother, Hades. The dead lived here, their spirits ferried over from the land of the living by a fiery-eyed boatman, Charon.

The entrance to the Underworld was guarded by a fierce three-headed dog named Cerberus. He made sure that no one escaped.

Very rarely, someone got past Cerberus by lulling him to sleep. Beautiful music worked, as did drugged honey-cakes.

The Underworld was surrounded by a river, which could only be crossed in Charon's boat. Charon always asked for a coin in exchange for carrying the dead. The Greeks put coins inside the mouths of dead people, so they would be able to pay him.

CERBERUS
19th-century English drawing by Edward Burne-Jones

CHARON CROSSING THE RIVER STYX
16th-century Dutch painting by Joachim Patenier

The Underworld was divided into three main parts. The dead ended up in different places, depending on what they had done during their lives.

Heroes and those loved by the gods went to a beautiful garden known as the Elysian Fields.

Ordinary people ended up in the drab, shadowy Asphodel Fields.

Evildoers were plunged into the dark pit of Tartarus.

PERSEPHONE

Hades fell in love with Persephone – daughter of the nature goddess, Demeter. He carried Persephone off to the Underworld and married her, without asking Demeter's permission. Demeter missed her daughter so much, she stopped making things grow.

Hades rode around in a chariot pulled by a team of magnificent, night-black horses.

Persephone was busy gathering flowers when the ground split open and Hades appeared to spirit her away.

THE FATE OF PERSEPHONE
19th-century English painting by Walter Crane

Eventually, Zeus decreed Persephone should divide her time between Demeter and Hades. Each year, the months Persephone spent in the Underworld brought the winter, while her return marked the start of spring.

Persephone ate a few pomegranate seeds in the Underworld. For each seed, she had to spend a month of the year there.

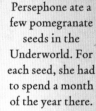

PERSEPHONE
Detail of Roman wall painting
1st-3rd century

ORPHEUS

Orpheus was famous for his music, which charmed all who heard it – even the animals.

When Orpheus' wife died, he followed her to the Underworld and tried to win her back with music. He played so beautifully, Hades agreed to let her go – on the condition that Orpheus didn't look back. Unfortunately he did, and lost her forever.

ORPHEUS PLAYING TO THE ANIMALS
Roman mosaic, 3rd century

JASON AND THE GOLDEN FLEECE

JASON WAS A PRINCE WHO, to claim his throne, had to sail in search of the fabled Golden Fleece on his ship, the *Argo*. A brave band of friends and sailors, known as the Argonauts, accompanied him.

The Argo was made partly of magical wood and was able to speak.

THE ARGO
16th-century Italian painting by Lorenzo Costa

Along the way, the Argonauts landed on the island of King Phineas. He was being plagued by monstrous birds called harpies. Anything he tried to eat, the harpies snatched away – until the Argonauts chased them away.

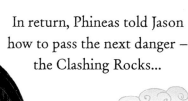

In return, Phineas told Jason how to pass the next danger – the Clashing Rocks...

The harpies had women's heads, with eagles' wings and feet.

HARPY
Greek vase,
6th century BC

PASSING THROUGH THE CLASHING ROCKS
16th-century Italian ceiling painting

To find the Golden Fleece, Jason had to get to Colchis. The Clashing Rocks towered over the route, smashing together when anything passed between them.

Jason tested them by sending through a dove. It got past, losing just a few tail feathers. So the Argonauts followed – and lost just the tail-end of their ship.

Before parting with the Golden Fleece, the King of Colchis gave Jason three tasks. The king thought the tasks were impossible. But his daughter, Medea, decided to help the handsome prince...

JASON AND MEDEA
Early 20th-century English painting by John William Waterhouse

① The first task was to till a field using two fire-breathing bulls. Medea gave Jason a magic ointment to keep him from being burned.

Jason reaches up for the fleece - which came from a magical flying sheep.

JASON ABOUT TO SEIZE THE GOLDEN FLEECE
Greek vase, 5th century BC

② The next task was to sow a bag of dragons' teeth. The teeth grew into soldiers who attacked Jason. On Medea's advice, he threw a rock at them – which made them turn on each other.

③ The third task was to defeat the dragon which guarded the Golden Fleece. Medea gave Jason a potion which sent it to sleep. Then, he took the fleece and escaped with Medea.

On the way back, the Argonauts had to pass the Sirens – sea monsters with human faces, who sang to lure sailors to their deaths. But one of the Argonauts, Orpheus (see page 19), sang even more beautifully and drowned out their song.

Jason eventually returned with the Golden Fleece to claim the throne.

This siren has a fish-like tail, but Greek artists usually showed them with the bodies of birds.

SIREN
Etruscan bronze sculpture, 6th century BC

THE TASKS OF HERACLES

THE GREEK HERO HERACLES (Hercules to the Romans) had to perform 12 tasks, to earn the gods' forgiveness for killing his children in a fit of insanity. The tasks were designed to be as hard as possible...

(1) First, Heracles had to kill the savage Nemean lion. Weapons bounced off the lion's fur, so he strangled it with his bare hands – and kept its skin as a cloak.

HERACLES AND THE NEMEAN LION
Roman carving, 1st century BC

(2) Next he had to slay a nine-headed monster known as the Hydra. Each time he cut off one head, two grew in its place – until his nephew stepped in and burned the stumps.

(3) Then he had to catch a golden deer belonging to the goddess Artemis.

(4) He had to catch a giant wild boar.

(5) Next, he had to clean the stables of King Augeas in a day. The stables were so huge and so dirty, he diverted a river to wash them clean.

HERACLES AND THE AUGEAN STABLES
Roman mosaic, 3rd century

(6) The Stymphalian Birds were man-eating birds with metal beaks and feathers. Heracles had to kill them.

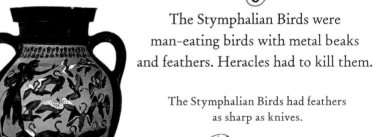

The Stymphalian Birds had feathers as sharp as knives.

STYMPHALIAN BIRDS
Greek vase,
6th century BC

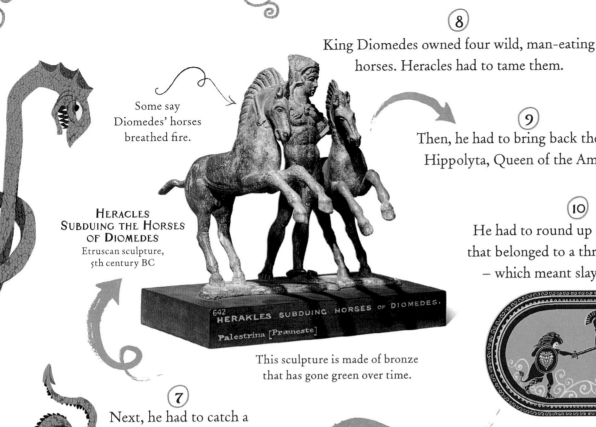

(8) King Diomedes owned four wild, man-eating horses. Heracles had to tame them.

Some say Diomedes' horses breathed fire.

HERACLES SUBDUING THE HORSES OF DIOMEDES
Etruscan sculpture,
5th century BC

This sculpture is made of bronze that has gone green over time.

(9) Then, he had to bring back the belt of Hippolyta, Queen of the Amazons.

(10) He had to round up a herd of cattle that belonged to a three-headed giant – which meant slaying the giant.

(7) Next, he had to catch a ferocious wild bull.

(11) He had to steal the golden apples of the Hesperides – guarded by three beautiful maidens and a hundred-headed dragon.

The golden apples belonged to Hera. Eating them made you live forever.

GARDEN OF THE HESPERIDES
19th-century English painting
by Frederick Leighton

(12) His last task was to bring back Cerberus, the three-headed dog, from the Underworld.

Cerberus terrified the king setting the tasks. He was so scared, he hid inside a pot and let Heracles go free.

HERACLES DRAGGING CERBERUS
18th-century Italian painting
by Domenico Pedrini

FOOLISH MORTALS

MANY GREEK MYTHS tell of ordinary, mortal men and women who foolishly challenged or disobeyed the gods – and often came to a sticky end.

PANDORA

Pandora was the first mortal woman. The gods gave her a box and told her never to open it (although they knew she would). When she lifted the lid, all the troubles of the world flew out. But she managed to hold onto hope, which was in the box too.

PANDORA
19th-century English drawing
by Dante Gabriel Rossetti

Zeus (seen here riding an eagle) knocked Phaethon out of the sky, to keep the runaway Sun from burning the Earth.

PHAETHON

Phaethon was the son of Helios, the god who drove the Sun across the sky in his chariot, and a mortal woman. Phaethon insisted he could take his father's place. But the chariot ran away with him and he fell to his death.

THE FALL OF PHAETHON
16th-century Italian drawing by
Michelangelo Buonarroti

MIDAS

When Dionysus granted King Midas a wish, the greedy king asked for everything he touched to turn to gold. But he begged to undo his wish when his food and drink hardened before it reached his mouth.

KING MIDAS
20th-century English book illustration
by Arthur Rackham

SISYPHUS

King Sisyphus was always scheming. He even tried to trick his way out of dying. In punishment, Zeus made him roll a boulder uphill forever. Each time he neared the top, it would roll down again.

ARACHNE

Arachne boasted she could weave better than anyone, even Athena. So the goddess challenged her to a contest. Arachne daringly wove a tapestry showing the faults of the gods – and the furious Athena changed her into a spider.

CASSANDRA

Apollo gave Cassandra the gift of seeing the future. Then, when she broke a promise, he added the catch that no one would believe her. The burden of her knowledge eventually drove her insane.

Cassandra knew her city would be destroyed – but no one believed her, so she couldn't do anything about it.

THE FABLE OF ARACHNE
17th-century Spanish painting by Diego Velasquez

Icarus stands proudly on a pedestal to show off his new wings.

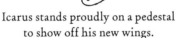

ICARUS

Icarus and his father, Daedalus, were locked in a tower. Daedalus was an inventor, and made wax and feather wings so they could fly away. But Icarus flew too high, the sun melted his wings and he fell...

ICARUS AND HIS FATHER
Roman carving, 1st century

This picture shows just the end of the story – with a splash and a pair of legs disappearing – while ordinary people go about their lives unaware.

LANDSCAPE WITH THE FALL OF ICARUS
16th-century Flemish painting by Pieter Bruegel

METAMORPHOSES

SOME VERY FAMOUS GREEK MYTHS involve people being magically transformed into other shapes or forms – known as metamorphoses.

DAPHNE

Apollo fell in love with Daphne, a nymph (see page 16), but she ran away. She asked a river god to help her escape, and he turned her into a laurel tree. Apollo wore a crown of laurel leaves ever after.

This picture captures the moment as Daphne begins to change.

APOLLO AND DAPHNE
15th-century Italian painting
by Antonio del Pollaiuolo

ACTAEON

Actaeon was out hunting one day when he stumbled on Artemis bathing in a lake. Furious, Artemis changed him into a stag – and his own dogs chased him down.

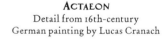

ACTAEON
Detail from 16th-century
German painting by Lucas Cranach

ATALANTA

Speedy Atalanta refused to marry until she found a suitor who could win a race against her. No one could – until Melanion. Each time Atalanta got ahead of him, he dropped a golden apple to distract her.

ATALANTA AND MELANION
19th-century English painting by John Batten

The two were married and lived happily until they failed to respect the gods – and were changed into lions as a punishment.

PYGMALION

Pygmalion made a sculpture of a woman and fell in love with her. He prayed to Aphrodite to bring her to life, so he could marry her. Then he kissed her – and found her warm. The goddess had granted his wish.

In later retellings, the statue who came to life was named Galatea.

GALATEA
19th-century French sculpture by Auguste Rodin

NARCISSUS

Handsome Narcissus was so vain, he fell in love with his reflection in a pool of water. He stayed by the pool until he wasted away and died. After his death, the gods turned him into a narcissus flower.

NARCISSUS
16th-century Italian painting by Caravaggio

ECHO

The nymph Echo annoyed Hera with her constant chatter. So Hera cursed her to repeat only what others said. Eventually Echo faded away, until she was just a voice on the wind.

Echo had a beautiful voice, and was always singing or telling stories.

ADONIS

Adonis was so handsome, Aphrodite herself fell in love with him. When he died after being attacked by a boar, she changed his blood into anemones – a flower that lives for only a short time.

Doves were one of the symbols of Aphrodite.

The 'Adonis' anemone has blood-red flowers.

THE AWAKENING OF ADONIS
19th-century English painting by John William Waterhouse

Aphrodite is attended by pretty children, including her son, Eros.

THE TROJAN WAR

ONE MAJOR GREEK MYTH, retold many times, tells of the battles between the Greeks and the Trojans, who went to war over a beautiful queen named Helen.

It all began when Aphrodite promised Paris, Prince of Troy, the love of Helen, the world's most beautiful woman (see page 7). Aphrodite made Helen fall in love and run away with Paris.

Paris escorts Helen to a waiting ship.

THE ABDUCTION OF HELEN OF TROY
17th-century Italian painting by Cesare Dandini

Helen's legendary beauty has fascinated artists for centuries.

HELEN ON THE RAMPARTS OF TROY
19th-century French painting by Gustave Moreau

Helen had many suitors, but her father thought King Menelaus was the best match.

Unfortunately, Helen was already married to King Menelaus of Greece. Menelaus and his brother, King Agamemnon, took their armies and went to bring her home. They set sail in a huge fleet.

MENELAUS
Roman stone bust, 2nd century

When they arrived, the armies laid siege to Troy. The siege lasted for ten years.

Hector was the brother of Paris. He led the Trojans bravely, even though he disapproved of the war.

Many brave warriors fought on both sides, including hot-tempered Achilles and mighty Ajax for the Greeks, and noble Hector for the Trojans.

AJAX ATTACKS HECTOR
detail of a Greek cup painted by Douris, 5th century BC

Hector (seen here on the right) challenged Ajax (on the left) to single combat.

Achilles was a mighty warrior. But, after arriving in Troy, he argued
with Agamemnon and refused to fight. Instead, one of his friends
borrowed his weapons and took his place – only to be killed
by Hector. Furious, Achilles went looking for revenge...

AJAX AND ACHILLES
Greek amphora by Exekias,
6th century BC

Achilles
(in the helmet)
and Ajax take
time from
fighting to play a
board game.

ACHILLES DEFEATING HECTOR
17th-century Flemish painting by Peter Paul Rubens

Athena watches over
the fight, accompanied
by her owl.

Achilles forces Hector
to the ground.

Achilles killed Hector. Then, still crazed with grief
for his friend, he tied Hector's body to his chariot
and dragged it around the walls of Troy. Hector's
father had to plead with Achilles in person
before it could be buried.

Eventually, a Greek named Odysseus
had a sneaky idea. The Greeks built
a huge wooden horse, and some
of their soldiers hid inside.

The Trojans thought the horse was an offering to the gods,
and brought it into their city. After dark, the Greek soldiers crept out
and opened the gates for the rest of their army. Then they ransacked the city.

Menelaus was finally
reunited with Helen,
and they sailed back
home together.

THE TROJAN HORSE 15th-century Italian painting

THE JOURNEY HOME

ANOTHER VERY FAMOUS GREEK MYTH follows the adventures of the warrior Odysseus, as he tried to make his way home after the Trojan War. Many obstacles lay in his way...

(1) After setting sail, Odysseus and his men were blown off course, to a land of one-eyed giants known as Cyclopes.

ODYSSEUS AND THE CYCLOPS
19th-century reproduction of an ancient Greek vase

(2) A Cyclops named Polyphemus trapped the men in a cave, so he could eat them. But they blinded him and escaped by clinging to his sheep when he let them out to graze.

(7) Odysseus washed up on the island where Calypso, a lonely nymph, lived. She kept him captive for seven years. Eventually, Athena intervened and Calypso let him go.

(6) Odysseus and his men found an island full of cattle belonging to the Sun god, Helios. Tired and hungry, the men ate the sacred cattle. As a punishment, their ship was wrecked.

(8) Odysseus finally made it home with the help of a seafaring people known as the Phaeacians. Guided by Athena, he went to see his wife, Penelope. He had been gone so long, most people thought he was dead. Penelope had been plagued by suitors.

THE RETURN OF ULYSSES
Detail of a panel from a 15th-century Italian chest; Ulysses is the Roman name for Odysseus.

Penelope refused to marry until she finished a tapestry. She wove it by day, and unpicked it at night.

③

Aeolus, keeper of the winds, gave Odysseus a bag of winds to blow him home. But his men tore it open and caused a storm. They were blown off course again, and were nearly killed by cannibals.

④

They landed on the island of a sorceress, Circe, who turned half the men into beasts. Odysseus charmed her into turning them back and telling him what he needed to do next...

CIRCE
20th-century French print
by Edmund Dulac

⑤

According to Circe, he had to talk to spirits from the Underworld. He had to sail past the Sirens (see page 21) without falling prey to their deadly song...

...and he had to steer his ship between the six-headed monster Scylla and a deadly whirlpool.

**ODYSSEUS
AND THE SIRENS**
Fragment of a Roman mosaic,
3rd century

To get past the Sirens, Odysseus was tied to the mast and his men blocked their ears with wax.

Odysseus came back disguised as a beggar, so Penelope's suitors wouldn't recognise him.

Each of Scylla's six heads seized a sailor – but the rest of the crew made it through safely.

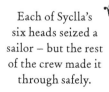

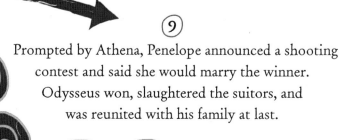

⑨

Prompted by Athena, Penelope announced a shooting contest and said she would marry the winner. Odysseus won, slaughtered the suitors, and was reunited with his family at last.

**ODYSSEUS
AND PENELOPE**
Greek stone
carving,
5th century BC

INDEX

ACKNOWLEDGEMENTS

Edited by Jane Chisholm. Art Director: Mary Cartwright.

COVER Fate of Persephone, see credit for pages 18-19. Wounded Chimera (bronze), see credit for pages 12-13. Amphora with Stymphalian Birds, see credit for pages 22-23. PAGES 2-3 Mount Olympus © Vanni Archive/ CORBIS. Attic black-figure neck-amphora © Christie's Images/ CORBIS. Birth of Venus by Sandro Botticelli © Corbis. Acropolis © Reed Kaestner/ Corbis. PAGES 4-5 Fountain of Saturn (Cronus), Chateau de Versailles, France/ Bridgeman Art Library. Fall of the Titans by Rubens © 2012 Photo Scala, Florence. Cyclops by Odilon Redon © Corbis. Statue of Atlas © Mimmo Jodice/ CORBIS. High Atlas Mountains © Radius Images/ Corbis. Attic red-figure calyx-krater with satyrs and Prometheus, Ashmolean Museum, University of Oxford, UK/ Bridgeman Art Library. Black-figure kylix with Atlas and Prometheus by the Arkesilas Painter, Vatican Museums and Galleries, Vatican City/ Bridgeman Art Library. PAGES 6-7 Laconian cup with Zeus and the eagle by the Naukratis Painter, Louvre, Paris, France/ Bridgeman Art Library. Neptune Calming the Waves by Lambert-Sigisbert Adam, Louvre, Paris, France/ Giraudon/ Bridgeman Art Library. Detail from Orpheus and Eurydice by Peter Paul Rubens, Prado, Madrid, Spain/ Giraudon/ Bridgeman Art Library. Detail of Juno with a peacock by Baldassarre Peruzzi, from the Hall of Perspective, Villa Farnesina, Rome, Italy/ Bridgeman Art Library. Venus de Milo © Bertrand Rieger/ Hemis/ Corbis. Red-figure krater with Triptolemus and Demeter by the Niobid Painter © Alfredo Dagli Orti/ Art Archive/ Corbis. Judgement of Paris by the Master of the Argonaut Panels, Fogg Art Museum, Harvard University Art Museums, USA/ Gift of Meta and Paul J. Sachs/ Bridgeman Art Library. PAGES 8-9 Silver coin with head of Athena © Trustees of the British Museum. All rights reserved. Pallas Athena by Gustav Klimt © Gallery Collection/ Corbis. Apollo by Pietro Perugino, Salla del Cambio, Perugia, Italy/ Bridgeman Art Library. Diana the Huntress (fresco), Museo Archeologico Nazionale, Naples, Italy/ Index/ Bridgeman Art Library. Attic red-figure lekythos with Apollo and Artemis and a deer, Ashmolean Museum, University of Oxford, UK/ Bridgeman Art Library. Ludovisi Ares © Mimmo Jodice/ CORBIS. Terracotta lekythos with Hermes © Metropolitan Museum of Art/ Art Resource/ Scala, Florence. PAGES 10-11 Theseus fighting the Minotaur by Antoine Louis Barye, Dayton Art Institute, Dayton, Ohio, USA/ Museum purchase with funds provided by the James F. Dicke Family in memory of Timothy M. Webster/ Bridgeman Art Library. Infant Hercules strangling Serpents © Araldo de Luca/ CORBIS. Perseus Rescuing Andromeda by Piero di Cosimo © Summerfield Press/ CORBIS. Bellerophon Riding Pegasus Fighting the Chimaera by Peter Paul Rubens, Musee Bonnat, Bayonne, France/ Giraudon/ Bridgeman Art Library. Statue of Atalanta, Louvre, Paris, France/ Giraudon/ Bridgeman Art Library. Labours of Psyche by John Roddam Spencer Stanhope, Private Collection/ Photo © Peter Nahum at Leicester Galleries, London/ Bridgeman Art Library. PAGES 12-13 Chalcidian black-figure hydria with Typhon, Staatliche Antikensammlungen und Glyptothek, Munchen (Munich), photo by Renate Kuhling. Roman Sphinx, Colchester Castle Museum, Colchester, Essex, UK/ Ancient Art and Architecture Collection Ltd./ Bridgeman Art Library. Red-figure volute krater with Orestes and the Furies, Musee Municipal, Laon, France/ Giraudon/ Bridgeman Art Library. Drawing of Three Fates by Henry Moore, reproduced by permission of The Henry Moore Foundation; photo © Burstein Collection/ CORBIS. Medusa by Michelangelo Merisi da Caravaggio © Arte & Immagini srl/ CORBIS. Wounded Chimera of Bellerophon (bronze), Museo Archeologico, Florence, Italy/ Bridgeman Art Library. PAGES 14-15 Detail of the Three Graces from Primavera by Sandro Botticelli © Alfredo Dagli Orti/ Art Archive/ Corbis. Griffin head, fragment of a cauldron attachment, Louvre, Paris, France/ Bridgeman Art Library. Young Centaur by Papias of Aphrodisias © Araldo de Luca/ CORBIS. Faun, Ferens Art Gallery, Hull Museums, UK/ Bridgeman Art Library. Mosaic of Nine Muses, Rheinisches Landesmuseum, Trier, Germany/ De Agostini Picture Library/ A. Dagli Orti/ Bridgeman Art Library. Black Pegasus by Odilon Redon, Private Collection/ Photo © Christie's Images/ Bridgeman Art Library. PAGES 16-17 Dryad by Evelyn de Morgan © De Morgan Centre, London/ Bridgeman Art Library. Pan by Annibale Carracci, National Gallery of Victoria, Melbourne, Australia/ Felton Bequest/ Bridgeman Art Library. Omphalos (photo), Archaeological Museum, Delphi, Greece/ Bernard Cox/ Bridgeman Art Library. Map of the Northern Constellations by Sir James Thornhill © Stapleton Collection/ Corbis. Detail from Birth of Venus by Sandro Botticelli © Corbis. PAGES 18-19 Story of Orpheus: Cerberus by Sir Edward Burne-Jones, Ashmolean Museum, University of Oxford, UK/ Bridgeman Art Library. Landscape With Charon's Boat © Francis G. Mayer/ CORBIS. Fate of Persephone by Walter Crane, Private Collection, Photo © Christie's Images/ Bridgeman Art Library. Detail of fresco with Persephone, Landesmuseum, Klagenfurt, Austria/ De Agostini Picture Library/ E. Lessing/ Bridgeman Art Library. Mosaic of Orpheus playing his Harp to Animals © Chris Hellier/ CORBIS. PAGES 20-21 Argo by Lorenzo Costa, Museo Civico, Padua, Italy/ Alinari/ Bridgeman Art Library. Black-figure amphora depicting a harpy, photo © BEBA/ AISA/ Bridgeman Art Library. Ship of the Argonauts Passing through the Symplegades © Photo Scala, Florence – courtesy of the Ministero Beni e Att. Culturali. Jason and Medea by John William Waterhouse, private collection, photo © Maas Gallery, London/ Bridgeman Art Library. Terracotta column-krater with Jason about to seize the Golden Fleece, image © Metropolitan Museum of Art/ Art Resource/ Scala, Florence. Etruscan Siren © David Lees/ CORBIS. PAGES 22-23 Cameo of Hercules and the Nemean Lion, Museo Archeologico Nazionale, Naples, Italy/ Bridgeman Art Library. Mosaic of Hercules and the Augean Stables, from 'House of Hercules', Volubilis, Morocco © Gerard Degeorge/ Bridgeman Art Library. Black-figured amphora with Stymphalian Birds © Trustees of the British Museum. All rights reserved. Hercules subduing the horses of Diomedes, British Museum, London, UK/ Bridgeman Art Library. Garden of the Hesperides by Frederic Leighton © Lady Lever Art Gallery, National Museums Liverpool/ Bridgeman Art Library. Hercules dragging Cerberus from Hell by Domenico Pedrini © Christie's Images/ CORBIS. PAGES 24-25 Pandora by Dante Gabriel Rossetti, Faringdon Collection, Buscot, Oxon, UK/ Bridgeman Art Library. Fall of Phaeton by Michelangelo Buonarroti, Royal Collection © 2011 Her Majesty Queen Elizabeth II/ Bridgeman Art Library. It struck Midas as rather inconvenient, illustration by Arthur Rackham, private collection/ Stapleton Collection/ Bridgeman Art Library. Spinners: Fable of Arachne by Diego Rodriquez de Silva y Velazquez © Art Archive/ Corbis. Cameo of Icarus and Daedalus, Museo Archeologico Nazionale, Naples, Italy/ Bridgeman Art Library. Landscape with the Fall of Icarus by Pieter Brueghel the Elder © Gallery Collection/ Corbis. PAGES 26-27 Apollo and Daphne by Antonio del Pollaiuolo © Corbis. Diana and Actaeon by Lucas Cranach the Elder © Fine Art Photographic Library/ CORBIS. Atalanta and Melanion by John Dickson Batten, private collection/ Bridgeman Art Library. Galatea by Auguste Rodin, Musee Rodin, Paris, France/ Philippe Galard/ Bridgeman Art Library. Narcissus by Caravaggio, Palazzo Barberini, Rome, Italy/ Bridgeman Art Library. Awakening of Adonis by John William Waterhouse, private collection, photo © Maas Gallery, London/ Bridgeman Art Library. PAGES 28-29 Abduction of Helen of Troy by Cesare Dandini, private collection, photo © Bonhams, London, UK/ Bridgeman Art Library. Helen on the Ramparts of Troy by Gustave Moreau, Musee Gustave Moreau, Paris, France/ Giraudon/ The Bridgeman Art Library. Bust of Menelaus, Vatican Museums and Galleries, Vatican City, Italy/ Alinari/ Bridgeman Art Library. Detail from Attic red-figure cup ('The Douris Cup') by Kalliades, with Ajax, urged by Athena, attacking Hector, Louvre, Paris, France/ Bridgeman Art Library. Black-figure amphora with Ajax and Achilles by Exekias, Vatican Museums and Galleries, Vatican City, Italy/ Bridgeman Art Library. Achilles Defeating Hector by Peter Paul Rubens, Musee des Beaux-Arts, Pau, France/ Giraudon/ Bridgeman Art Library. Trojan Horse, Musee National de la Renaissance, Ecouen, France/ Giraudon/ Bridgeman Art Library. PAGES 30-31 Circe by Edmund Dulac © Christie's Images/ CORBIS. Ulysses and his companions gouging out the eye of the Cyclops, illustration from an antique Greek vase, 1887 (colour litho), Bibliotheque des Arts Decoratifs, Paris, France/ Archives Charmet/ Bridgeman Art Library. Return of Ulysses, cassone panel, Musee National de la Renaissance, Ecouen, France/ Giraudon/ Bridgeman Art Library. Mosaic with Ulysses and the Sirens, Musee du Bardo, Tunis, Tunisia/ Giraudon/ Bridgeman Art Library. Relief with Odysseus and Penelope, Louvre, Paris, France/ Giraudon/ Bridgeman Art Library.

This edition first published in 2015 by Usborne Publishing Ltd.,
Usborne House, 83-85 Saffron Hill, London EC1N 8RT, England. www.usborne.com
Copyright © 2015, 2012 Usborne Publishing Ltd. UE.